W9-CLO-989

Text: © 2007 David LaMotte
Illustrations: © 2012 Jenn Hales

All rights reserved. No portion of this book may be reproduced in any form without written permission of the publisher and author. Please direct inquiries for permission to booking@davidlamotte.com.

ISBN-10: 097728932X
ISBN-13: 978-0-9772893-2-5

Library of Congress Control Number: 2012905832

The illustrator, Jenn Hales, created the art for this book by painting on birch wood panels with layered glazes of acrylic paint.

ENVIRONMENTAL BENEFITS STATEMENT

Lower Dryad Music saved the following resources by printing the pages of this book on chlorine free paper made with 10% post-consumer waste.

TREES	WATER	ENERGY	SOLID WASTE	GREENHOUSE GASES
4	1,497	1	95	331
FULLY GROWN	GALLONS	MILLION BTUs	POUNDS	POUNDS

Environmental impact estimates were made using the Environmental Paper Network Paper Calculator. For more information visit www.papercalculator.org.

Printed by Friesens — friesens.com
Art scans by Artful Color — artfulcolor.com
Book Layout and Design by Jenn Hales.

Made in Canada.

10 9 8 7 6 5 4 3 2 1

Published by Lower Dryad Music
David LaMotte • davidlamotte.com
Jenn Hales • jennhales.com
White Flour • whiteflourbook.com

Hickory, North Carolina
Patrick Beaver Memorial Library
Hickory, NC 28601

White Flour

written by David LaMotte

illustrated by Jenn Hales

DiPietro Library
Franklin Pierce University
Rindge, NH 03461

The day was bright and sunny as most May days tend to be
In the hills of Appalachia down in Knoxville, Tennessee

A dozen men put on their suits and quickly took their places
In white robes and those tall and pointed hoods that hid their faces

Their feet fell down in rhythm as they started their parade
They raised their fists into the air, they bellowed and they brayed

They loved to stir the people up, they loved when they were taunted
They didn't mind the anger, it's exactly what they wanted

As they came around the corner, sure enough the people roared
But they couldn't quite believe their ears, it seemed to be support!
Had Knoxville finally seen the light? Were people coming 'round?
The men thought for a moment that they'd found their kind of town

But then they turned their eyes to where the cheering had its source
As one their shoulders crumpled when they saw the mighty force

The crowd had painted faces and some had tacky clothes
Their hair and hats outrageous, each had a bright red nose
The clowns had come in numbers to enjoy the grand parade
They laughed and danced that other clowns had come to town that day

And then the marchers shouted, and the clowns all strained to hear
Each one tuned in intently with a hand cupped to an ear
"White power!" screamed the marchers, and they raised their fisted hands
The clowns leaned in and listened like they couldn't understand

Then one held up his finger and helped all the others see
The point of all this yelling, and they joined right in with glee...

"White flour!" the clowns shouted, and they reached inside their clothes
They pulled out bags and tore them and huge clouds of powder rose
They poured it on each other and they threw it in the air
It got all over baggy clothes and multi-colored hair

Now all but just a few of them were joining in the jokes
You could almost see the marchers turning red beneath white cloaks
They wanted to look scary! They wanted to look tough!
One rushed right at the clowns in rage and was hauled away in cuffs

But the others chanted louder, marching on around the bend
The clowns all marched on too, of course, supporting their new friends
"White power!" came the marchers' cry, they were not amused
The clowns grew still and thoughtful—well, perhaps they'd been confused...?

They huddled and consulted, this bright and silly crowd
They listened quite intently, then one said "I've got it now!"

"White flowers!" screamed the happy clown, and all the rest joined in
The air was filled with flowers, and they laughed and danced again
"Everyone loves flowers, and white's a pretty sort
I can't think of a better cause for people to support!"

Green flower stems went flying like small arrows from bad archers
White petals covered everything, including the mad marchers

And then a very tall clown called the others to attention
He choked down all his chuckles and said "Friends I have to mention
That what with all this mirth and fun it's sort of hard to hear
But now I know the cause that these paraders hold so dear!"

"Tight showers!" the clown blurted, as he hit his head in wonder
He held up a camp shower and the others all got under
Or at least they tried to get beneath, they strained but couldn't quite
There wasn't room for all of them, they pushed, but it was tight!

"White Power!" came the mad refrain, quite carefully pronounced
The clowns consulted once again, then a woman clown announced
"I've got it! I'm embarrassed that it took so long to see,
But what these marchers march for is a cause quite dear to me!"

"Wife power!" she exclaimed, and all the other clowns joined in
They shook their heads and laughed at how erroneous they'd been
The women clowns were hoisted up on shoulders of the others
Some pulled on wedding dresses, chanting "Here's to wives and mothers!"

The men in robes were sullen, they knew they'd been defeated
They yelled a few more times and then they finally retreated

And when they'd gone a kind policeman turned to all the clowns
And offered them an escort through the center of the town

The day was bright and sunny as most May days tend to be
In the hills of Appalachia down in Knoxville, Tennessee
People joined the new parade, the crowd stretched out for miles
The clowns passed out more flowers and made everybody smile

And what would be the lesson of that shiny southern day?
Can we understand the message that the clowns sought to convey?
Seems that when you're fighting hatred, hatred's not the thing to use!

so here's to those who march on...

...in their big red floppy shoes

About the Illustrator

As a child Jenn Hales spent her time reading books and examining bumble-bees in the front yard. Her family didn't have a tv, so she drew the creatures she saw in nature and in her imagination.

Later, Jenn moved to Ohio where she graduated from the University of Cincinnati with a degree in Industrial Design. She's worked as a toy designer at Hasbro, a footwear designer at Columbia sportswear, a design researcher at Insight Product Development, and a welder at SAS institute.

Nowadays, Jenn lives in Raleigh, NC and works as a full time illustrator and artist. When she's not painting she spends her time with her partner Graymon and her dog Totoro.

You can find more about Jenn Hales and her work at jennhales.com

About the Author

David LaMotte is a dad, a husband, an itinerant peace guy, a lover of garlic, a poet and a very bad racquetball player. He makes his living as a singer/songwriter and a public speaker, sometimes at the same time. He has led workshops, keynoted and performed well over 2000 concerts on four continents, and put out ten CDs over the last twenty years. He is also a Rotary World Peace Fellow with a masters in International Studies, Peace and Conflict Resolution from the University of Queensland in Brisbane, Australia. For hobbies, he is the co-founder and unpaid director of a small non-profit that works with schools and libraries in Guatemala, PEG Partners, and the Clerk (chair) of the AFSC Nobel Peace Prize Nomination Committee, which chooses a nominee to put forward each year on behalf of Quakers, who, as Nobel laureates (1947), have the privilege of nominating.

White Flour is his second children's book. S.S. Bathtub, based on his award-winning song by the same name and illustrated by Carrie Patterson, is a rhyming book for younger kids. He is currently working on a non-fiction book for adults, tentatively titled Worldchanging 101: Challenging the Myth of Powerlessness, which is also a frequent topic for his talks.

He has lived in Florida, Virginia, North Carolina, France, Australia and India, but he likes everywhere else, too. Currently, he lives in Chapel Hill, North Carolina, with his wife Deanna and son Mason.

Should you need help procrastinating, there's free streaming music, video and lots more about him and what he's up to on his website, davidlamotte.com.

This book is inspired by the Coup Clutz Clown activists, from Mountain Justice and other organizations, who originally conceived of this clever and effective action, then carried it out. Our profound gratitude and respect to them.

Major Backers
Deepest gratitude to the 592 backers that supported the first printing of this book through kickstarter.com. Special thanks to the following major backers:

Carmichael Presbyterian Church, Carmichael, CA
Dave & Jackie Henry
Kathy LaMotte
Eric Jackson
Rabbi Lisa Tzur
Bob and Pat Shufeldt
John & Olivia LaMotte
Lee & PJ Harris
Megan Livengood
& an anonymous backer, in honor of Henry Earl & June Woodall

Author Thanks
Many thanks to Barbie Angell, Lyndon Harris, Sarah Hipp, Laura Hope-Gill, Kathy LaMotte, Chris Liu-Beers, Flip Lower, Sarah Mahoney, Geoff McGlashan, Julie Miles, Billy Oxford, Sherri Powers, George Reed, Joe Rhatigan, Jennifer Robenalt, David Sardinha, Scott Webber and Andrea Webster for their various forms of support of this project, as well as to Joanne L. Zysk, who originally shared the true story of the Coup Clutz Clowns with me. And special thanks to my wife, Deanna LaMotte, for supporting my dreams and for courageously dreaming her own, then following them (and letting me come along too).

Illustrator Thanks
Thank you to Graymon, Mom & Dad, Rachel Wilson, Amy, and all the folks at Blake Street.
And to Jaguar, Cuda, Leila, and Robin for posing.

Author Dedication
This book is dedicated to Mason Bishop LaMotte. Mason, you get to decide who you will become each day, but our sending prayer for you is that you will be one who builds— relationships, dreams, hope, peace, as a mason builds with stone. There's a place for demolition, but the more important work is building.

Illustrator Dedication
To Chilson.

Also available from David LaMotte:

S.S. Bathtub children's book and songs

Find out more at davidlamotte.com

Franklin Pierce University

00218717

DATE DUE

PRINTED IN U.S.A.